STUDENTS AT THE BRITISH SCHOOL AT ATHENS (1886-1914)

Compiled by
DAVID W.J. GILL

Swansea: The Ostraka Press
2008

Published by The Ostraka Press

ISBN 978-0-9558498-0-0

David W.J. Gill
Centre for Egyptology and Mediterranean
    Archaeology (CEMA)
School of Humanities
Swansea University
Swansea SA2 8PP
Wales – UK
www.swan.ac.uk/classics

CONTENTS

A. INTRODUCTION

The British School at Athens (BSA) admitted its first student (Ernest A. Gardner) in 1886. The subsequent thirty years saw a shift towards scientific and professional archaeology. The School developed a number of major projects: the Cyprus Exploration Fund; Megalopolis; Phylakopi on Melos; Laconia (and Sparta); Crete (Praisos, Palaikastro). Its members were also involved in the epigraphic surveys of the Asia Minor Exploration Fund, and the search for prehistoric sites through the Macedonian Exploration Fund. Many of the students who gained the experience of excavating in Greece were to work in the Levant, Egypt, India and Britain.

Students of the BSA have a specific meaning under the Rules and Regulations of the School. They are defined as:

XIX. The Students shall consist of the following:—

(1) Holders of travelling fellowships, studentships, or scholarships at any University of the United Kingdom or of the British Colonies.

(2) Travelling Students sent out by the Royal Academy, the Royal Institute of British Architects, or other similar bodies.

(3) Other persons who shall satisfy the Managing Committee that they are duly

> qualified to be admitted to the privileges of the School.
>
> XX. Students attached to the School will be expected to pursue some definite course of study or research in a department of Hellenic studies, and to write in each season a report upon their work ....
>
> XXI. ... No person shall be enrolled as a student who does not intend to reside at least three months in Greek lands.

These Rules and Regulations were updated to include mention of the British School at Rome:

> XX. No person, other than a student of the British School at Rome, shall be admitted as a Student who does not intend to reside at least three months in Greek lands. In the case of Students of the British School at Rome, an aggregate residence of four months at the two Schools will be accepted as alternative to three months' residence in Greece.

From the session 1903/04 a number of BSA students spent part of their year abroad in Rome as well as in Greece.

This project on individual students has grown out of research on the donors of Greek and Roman antiquities at the Fitzwilliam Museum, Cambridge, and the preparation (and revision) of entries for the *Oxford Dictionary of National Biography* (2004) and *The Dictionary of British Classicists* (2004). This work has shown that institutional histories of the BSA have placed an emphasis on the major personalities and have perhaps overlooked the contributions made by less well-known individuals.

The results of this research will appear in a major study of the British School at Athens from 1886 until the end of the First World War (though no new students were admitted in the formal sense during the war years).

This research would have been impossible without the help and support of Amalia Kakissis, archivist of the BSA, as well as the generosity of the numerous college, university and school archivists who have willingly provided information. Other colleagues have provided encouragement and support, sometimes unknowingly. These include Christopher A. Stray, Paul Bahn, Mark Curthoys, and Michael Vickers.

SELECT BIBLIOGRAPHY

Baker-Penoyre, J. 1910/11. Bibliography of the work of students, coming within the scope of the school's work but not published in the School Annual. *Annual of the British School at Athens* 17: xxxix-liv.

Beard, M., and C. Stray. 2005. The Academy abroad: the nineteenth-century origin of the British School Athens. In *The organisation of knowledge in Victorian Britain*, edited by M. J. Daunton, pp. 371-87. Oxford: British Academy and Oxford University Press.

Calligas, E., and J. Whitley (eds.) 2005. *On site: British archaeologists in Greece*. Athens: Motibo.

Dyson, S. L. 2006. *In pursuit of ancient pasts: a history of classical archaeology in the nineteenth and twentieth centuries*. New Haven: Yale University Press.

French, E. B. 1994. In the tracks of the British School in Laconia. In *Travellers and officials in the Peloponnese: descriptions-reports-statistics. In honour of Sir Steven Runciman*, pp. 297-302. Monemvasia: Monemvasiotikos Omilos.

Gill, D. W. J. 2000. Collecting for Cambridge: John Hubert Marshall on

Crete. *Annual of the British School at Athens* 95: 517-26.

—. 2002. "The passion of hazard": women at the British School at Athens before the First World War. *Annual of the British School at Athens* 97: 491-510.

—. 2004. The British School at Athens and archaeological research in the late Ottoman Empire. In *Archaeology, anthropology and heritage in the Balkans and Anatolia: the life and times of F.W. Hasluck, 1878-1920*, edited by D. Shankland, pp. 223-55, vol. 1. Istanbul: The Isis Press.

Huxley, D. (ed.) 2000. *Cretan quests: British explorers, excavators and historians*. London: British School at Athens.

Macmillan, G. A. 1910/11. A short history of the British School at Athens. 1886-1911. *Annual of the British School at Athens* 17: ix-xxxviii.

Megaw, A. H. S. 1988. "The British School at Athens and Cyprus." *Report of the Department of Antiquities Cyprus*: 281-86.

Stray, C. 2002. "The pen is mightier than the spade: archaeology and education in nineteenth century England." *Pharos* 10: 123-34.

Waterhouse, H. 1986. *The British School at Athens: the first hundred years*. British School at Athens supplementary volume, vol. 19. London: Thames & Hudson.

B. School Backgrounds

Aberdeen, Robert Gordon's College
Calder, William Moir. 1894-99.

Albany Academy, Glasgow
Fyfe, David Theodore.

Aldenham
Sikes, Edward Ernest.
Tillard, Laurence Berkley. 1902-06.

Ascot, St George's
Ormerod, Henry Arderne.

Ayr Academy
Edgar, Campbell Cowan.

Bath College
Frost, Kingdon Tregosse.

Birkenhead
Duckworth, Wynfrid Laurence Henry.

Blackheath
Guillemard, Francis Henry Hill.

Bradfield College
Lawson, John Cuthbert.

Cambridge, Leys
Hasluck, Frederick William.

CAMBRIDGE, PERSE
Stokes, John Laurence.
Tillyard, Eustace Mandeville
Wetenhall.

CANTERBURY, KING'S SCHOOL
Wigram, Rev. William Ainger.

CHARTERHOUSE
Doll, Christian Charles Tyler.
Munro, John Arthur Ruskin.
Oppé, Adolph Paul.
Parry, Oswald Hutton. Scholar.
Stokes, John Laurence.

CHEAM SCHOOL
Bevan, Edwyn Robert.

CHELTENHAM COLLEGE
Baker, Francis Brayne (Brayne-Baker).
Penoyre, John ff. Baker.

CITY OF LONDON SCHOOL
Fotheringham, John Knight.
Gardner, Ernest Arthur.
Hawes, Charles Henry.
Morrison, Frederick Arthur Charles.

CLIFTON COLLEGE
Edmonds, Charles Douglas.
Robinson, Edward Stanley Gotch.
Rodeck, Pieter.

CROSBY, MERCHANT TAYLORS' SCHOOL
See Merchant Taylors' School, Crosby.

DINAN, L'ÉCOLE LIBRE DES CORDELIERS, BRITTANY, FRANCE
Duckworth, Wynfrid Laurence Henry.

DULWICH COLLEGE
Comyn, Charles Heaton Fitzwilliam.
Hopkinson, John Henry. 1890-July 1895.
Marshall, John Hubert. 1887-July 1895.

DUNDEE HIGH SCHOOL
Lorimer, (Elizabeth) Hilda Lockhart.

ELGIN ACADEMY
Hardie, Margaret Masson (Mrs F.W. Hasluck).

ETON
Bosanquet, Robert Carr. King's Scholar; 1883-90.
Inge, Charles Cuthbert. King's Scholar; January 1883 - July 1887.
James, Montague Rhodes. 1877.
Loring, William. King's Scholar; September 1879 - March 1884.
Mayor, Robert John Grote. King's Scholar; September 1882 - December 1887.
Piddington, John George (J.G. Smith). January 1882 - July 1888.

Sheepshanks, Arthur Charles.
December 1897 to March 1901.
Yorke, Vincent Wodehouse. Newcastle
Scholar, 1888; King's Scholar;
September 1882 - July 1888.

HAILEYBURY
Thompson, Maurice Scott. 1898-1903.
Welch, Francis Bertram. 1889-90.

HARROW
Gutch, Clement. Easter 1889-Summer
1894; an entrance scholar; a Neeld
Scholar (1893).
Hoare, Edward Barclay. Easter 1886-
Summer 1890.
Pirie-Gordon, Charles Harry Clinton,
of Buthlaw. September 1896-
Summer 1900.

HELENSBURGH, LARCHFIELD ACADEMY
Frazer, James George.

HERTFORD, CHRIST'S HOSPITAL
Spilsbury, Alfred John.

HULL, HYMERS COLLEGE
Farrell, Wilfrid Jerome.

INVERNESS , RAINING'S SCHOOL
Mackenzie, Duncan.

LAUSANNE, COLLÈGE CANTONAL,
Tillyard, Eustace Mandeville
Wetenhall.

LIVERPOOL COLLEGE
Caspari, Max Otto Bismark (Max
Cary).

LONDON, ST PAUL'S SCHOOL
See St Paul's School, London.

MAIDA VALE HIGH SCHOOL
Richter, Gisela Marie Augusta.

MANCHESTER, WOODLANDS SCHOOL
Hopkinson, John Henry. 1885-89.

MANCHESTER GRAMMAR SCHOOL
Milne, Joseph Grafton. c. 1881-c. 1885;
Langworthy scholarship.

MANCHESTER HIGH SCHOOL
Lamb, Dorothy (Mrs J. Reeve Brooke).

MARLBOROUGH COLLEGE
Benson, Edward Frederic. Foundation
Scholar. September 1881-July 1887.
Bickford-Smith, Roandeu Albert
Henry. February 1871-December
1874.
Crowfoot, John Winter. Foundation
Scholar. 1887-July 1982.
Dawkins, Richard Mcgillivray. 1884-90.
Droop, John Percival.

West, Hercules Henry. Foundation
Scholar. August 1871-July 1875.

MERCHANT TAYLORS' SCHOOL
Casson, Stanley.
Gomme, Arnold Wycombe.
Laistner, Max Ludwig Wolfram.
Tod, Marcus Niebuhr.

MERCHANT TAYLORS' SCHOOL, CROSBY
Budden, Lionel Bailey.
Peet, Thomas Eric.

MONKTON COMBE
Bevan, Edwyn Robert. Summer term
1885-Summer term 1888.

NORWICH, KING EDWARD VI GRAMMAR SCHOOL
Tillard, Laurence Berkley. 1889-1902.

OXFORD, MAGDALEN COLLEGE SCHOOL
Welch, Francis Bertram.

PRESTON GRAMMAR SCHOOL
Myres, John Linton. 1879.

RADLEY
Whatley, Norman.

RAMSGATE, SOUTH EASTERN COLLEGE (LATER ST LAWRENCE COLLEGE)

Webster, Erwin Wentworth.

REPTON

Lambert, Richard Stanton. Sept 1908-July 1912.

RICHMOND

Guillemard, Francis Henry Hill.

ROSSALL SCHOOL

Atkinson, Thomas Dinham.
Bather, Arthur George. Exhibitioner.
Cheetham, J. Milne (Sir).
Jones, Henry Stuart.

RUGBY

Darbishire, Robert Shelby.
Heath, Roger Meyrick.
Ormerod, Henry Arderne.
Richards, George Chatterton.

ST PAUL'S SCHOOL, LONDON

Smith, Solomon Charles Kaines.

SEDBERGH GRAMMAR SCHOOL

Woodhouse, William John.

SHREWSBURY

Wace, Alan John Bayard.
Woodward, Arthur Maurice.

SOUTHWARK, ST OLAVE'S GRAMMAR SCHOOL
Grose, Sidney Wilson.

SOUTHWOLD, ST FELIX SCHOOL
Radford, Evelyn.

STONY STRATFORD, ST PAUL'S COLLEGE
Brooks, John Ellingham.

TAUNTON COLLEGE SCHOOL
Clarke, Rupert Charles.

TONBRIDGE SCHOOL
Tillyard, Henry Julius Wetenhall.

UPPINGHAM
Earp, Frank (Francis) Russell.
Wells, Robert Douglas.

USHAW COLLEGE, NEAR DURHAM
Farrell, Wilfrid Jerome.

WAKEFIELD GRAMMAR SCHOOL
Scutt, Cecil Allison.

WELLINGTON
Forster, Edward Seymour.

WINCHESTER COLLEGE
Awdry, Herbert. Commoner; Sept. 1865.

Brown, Alexander Cradock Bolney.
Scholar; Sept. 1895-1901.
Cheesman, George Leonard. Scholar;
Sept. 1897-1903.
Dickins, Guy. Scholar; Sept. 1895-1900.
Halliday (Hoffmeister), William
Reginald. Scholar.
Hogarth, David George. Commoner;
1876-81.
Moss-Blundell, Cyril Bertram. 1904-10.
Myres, John Linton. Scholar; 1882.
Stainer, John Frederick Randall.
Toynbee, Arnold Joseph. Scholar; 1902.

WYCOMBE ABBEY SCHOOL
Lamb, Dorothy (Mrs J. Reeve Brooke).

C. CAMBRIDGE COLLEGES

CHRIST'S COLLEGE

Baker, Francis Brayne (Brayne-Baker). Pensioner (14 January 1887); Scholar (1887); Exhibitioner (1891); Class. Trip. Pt 1, 2.1 (1890); Pt 2, 2nd (1891); BA (1890); MA (1896).

Grose, Sidney Wilson. Exhibitioner (1905); Scholar (1907); Class. Trip. Pt 1, 1st div. 2 (1908); Pt 2, classical archaeology, 1st, distinction (1909).

CLARE COLLEGE

Scutt, Cecil Allison. Admitted (1908); Class. Trip. Pt 1, 1st div. 2 (1910); Medieval and Modern Languages, 2nd (1911); Class. Trip. Pt 2, 1st (1912).

EMMANUEL COLLEGE

Dawkins, Richard Mcgillivray. Pensioner (Oct. 1898); Scholar (1899); Class. Trip. Pt 1, 1st div.3 (1901), Pt 2, 1st, language, distinction (1902); BA (1901); MA (1905).

Edmonds, Charles Douglas. Pensioner (24 Mar. 24 1894); Scholar (1898); Class. Trip. Pt 1, 1st div. 3 (1897), Pt 2, 1st, history, (1898); BA 1897; MA 1901.

GIRTON COLLEGE

Hutton, Caroline Amy. Class. Trip. Pt 1, 3rd div. 2 (1882), Pt 2, 2nd (1883).

Kohler, O.C. (Mrs Charles Smith). Class. Trip. Pt 1, 3rd div. 1 (1898), Pt 2, 2nd (1899).

Lorimer, (Elizabeth) Hilda Lockhart. Scholarship (1893); Class. Trip. Pt 1, 1st div. 2 (1896).

Richter, Gisela Marie Augusta. Class. Trip. Pt 1, 2nd div 3 (1904).

Sellers, Eugénie (Mrs A. Arthur Strong). Class. Trip. Pt 1, 3rd div. 3 (1882)

GONVILLE & CAIUS COLLEGE

Gardner, Ernest Arthur. Admitted (1880); Scholar; Class. Trip. Pt 1, 1st (1882), Pt 2, 1st (1884).

Guillemard, Francis Henry Hill. Pensioner (Feb. 1, 1870); BA (1874); MA (1877); M.D. (1881).

Tillyard, Henry Julius Wetenhall. Admitted (1 October 1900); Scholar; Class. Trip. Pt 1, 1st (1902); Pt II, 1st Class, (1904); BA (1904); MA (1910).

JESUS COLLEGE

Duckworth, Wynfrid Laurence Henry. Exhibitioner (Apr. 1889); Scholar (1890); Nat. Sci. Trip. Pt 1, 1st (1892); Pt 2, 1st (1893); BA (1892); MA (1896); MD (1905); Sc.D. (1906).

Farrell, Wilfrid Jerome. Scholar (October 1901); Class. Trip. Pt 1, 1st

div. 2 (1904); Pt 2, 1st (1905); BA
(1904); MA (1909).

Laistner, Max Ludwig Wolfram. Senior
Open Scholar (21 October 1909);
Class. Trip. Pt 1, 1st (1911); Pt 2, 1st
(1912); BA (1912); MA (1919); Litt.D.
(by proxy, 28 April 1944).

Morrison, Frederick Arthur Charles.
Pensioner (1891); Class. Trip. Pt 1,
1st (1895); Pt 2, 1st (1896); BA 1895.

Tillyard, Eustace Mandeville
Wetenhall. Scholar (October 1908).
Class. Trip. Pt 1, 1st,div. 3 (1910); Pt
2, 1st (1911); BA (1911); MA (1915);
Litt.D. (1933).

KING'S COLLEGE

Bather, Arthur George. Scholar (8 Oct.
1887); Class. Trip. Pt 1, 1st (1889); Pt
2, 1st (1891); BA (1891); MA (1895).

Benson, Edward Frederic. Admitted (4
October 1887); Exhibitioner (1888);
Scholar (1890); Prizeman; Class.
Trip. Pt 1, 1st (1890); Pt 2, 1st (1891);
BA (1890); MA (1938).

Earp, Frank (Francis) Russell.
Admitted (Oct. 4, 1890);
Exhibitioner (1892); Scholar (1893);
Prizeman; Class. Trip. Pt 1, 1st
(1893); Pt 2, 1st (1894); BA (1893);
MA (1897).

Gutch, Clement. Scholar (Oct. 9, 1894);
Scholar (1897); Class. Trip. Pt 1, 1st
(1897); Pt 2, Greek and Roman

archaeology, 1st (1898); BA (1897); MA (1901).

Hasluck, Frederick William. Admitted (Oct. 12, 1897); Scholar (1899); Class. Trip. Pt 1, 1st (1899); Pt 2, 1st (1901); BA (1901); MA (1904).

James, Montague Rhodes. Scholar from Eton (Oct. 14, 1882); Carus Prize (1882); Bell Scholar (1883); Craven Scholar (1884); Jeremie Septuagint Prize (1884); Class. Trip. Pt 1, 1st (1884); Pt 2, 1st (1885); BA (1885); 1st Chancellor's Medal; MA (1889); Litt.D. (1895).

Loring, William. Scholar from Eton (Oct. 10, 1885); Bell Scholar (1886); Battie Scholar (1888); Chancellor's (Classical) Medal (equal) (1889); Class. Trip. Pt 1, 1st (1887); Pt 2, 1st (1889); BA (1889) MA (1893).

Marshall, John Hubert. Scholar (Oct. 9, 1895); Scholar (1898); Porson Prize (1898); Class. Trip. Pt 1, 1st (1898); Pt 2, 1st (1900); BA (1898); MA (1902); Litt.D. (1913).

Mayor, Robert John Grote. Scholar from Eton (Oct. 10, 1888); Bell Scholar (1889); Craven Scholar (1891); Senior Classic (1890); Class. Trip. Pt 2, 1st (1892); BA (1892); MA (1896).

Yorke, Vincent Wodehouse. Scholar from Eton (Oct. 10, 1888); Scholar (1891); Class. Trip. Pt 1, 1st (1891); Pt 2, 1st (1892); BA (1891); MA (1895).

MAGDALENE COLLEGE

Smith, Solomon Charles Kaines.
Pensioner (Aug. 1, 1895); Class.
Trip. Pt 2, 1st, archaeology (1899);
BA (1898); MA (1902).

NEWNHAM COLLEGE

Conway, Agnes Ethel (Hon. Mrs
Horsfall). 1903-07; History Trip. Pt
1, 2nd (1905); Pt 2, 2nd (1906).
Hardie, Margaret Masson (Mrs F.W.
Hasluck). Class. Trip. Pt 1, 1st div. 2
(1909).
Lamb, Dorothy (Mrs J. Reeve Brooke).
Class. Trip. Pt 1, 3rd div. 2 (1909); Pt
2, 1st archaeology (1910).
Radford, Evelyn. 1905-09; Class. Trip.,
Pt 1, 3rd div. 1 (1908); Pt 2, 1st
archaeology (1909).
Taylor, Mary Norah Luton (Mrs
M.N.L. Bradshaw). Class. Trip. Pt 1,
1st div. 3 (1912), Pt 2, 1st archaeology
(1913).
Welsh, Margery Katharine (Mrs A. M.
Daniel). Class. Trip. Pt 1, 1st div. 3
(1902), Pt 2, 1st archaeology (1903).

PEMBROKE COLLEGE

Lawson, John Cuthbert. Pensioner
(Oct. 1, 1893); Scholar; Class. Trip.
Pt 1, 1st (1896); Pt 2, 1st (1897); BA
(1896); Members' Prize (Latin
Essay) (1897); Craven Studentship
(1898, 1899); MA (1900).

Stokes, John Laurence. Admitted (Oct. 1899); Class. Trip. Pt 1, 1st; Pt 2, 2nd (1903); BA 1902; MA 1928.

Wace, Alan John Bayard. Admitted (Oct. 1898); Scholar; Class. Trip. Pt 1, 1st (1901); Pt 2, 1st (1902); BA (1901); Craven Student (1903); Prendergast Student (1902, 1904); MA (1906).

PETERHOUSE

Brooks, John Ellingham. Pensioner (1 Oct. 1883); BA (1886).

ST JOHN'S COLLEGE

Sikes, Edward Ernest. Pensioner (May 1, 1886); Bell Scholar (1887); Scholar (1888); Class. Trip. Pt 1, 1st (1889); Pt 2, 1st, archaeology (1890); BA (1889); Browne Medal (Latin Ode) (1889); MA (1893).

Tillard, Laurence Berkley. Admitted (1906); Class. Trip. Pt 1, 1st (1909); Pt 2, 1st, history (1910); BA (1909); tutor, E.E. Sikes.

TRINITY COLLEGE

Bickford-Smith, Roandeu Albert Henry. Pensioner (1 June 1878); Law, 2nd (1882); BA (1883); MA (1886).

Bosanquet, Robert Carr. Pensioner (17 June 1890); Scholar (1891); Class. Trip. Pt 1, 1st (1892); Pt 2, 1st (1894); BA (1894); MA (1898).

Doll, Christian Charles Tyler.
Pensioner (25 June 1898); BA (1901);
MA (1906).

Droop, John Percival. Admitted (1900).
Class. Trip. Pt 1, 2nd div. 1 (1904); Pt
2, 1st, archaeology (1905); BA 1904,
MA 1912.

Gomme, Arnold Wycombe. Class.
Trip. Pt 1, 1st (1907); Pt 2, 1st, with
distinction in archaeology (1908).

Frazer, James George. Admitted (1874-
78); Class. Trip. 1st (1878).

Hawes, Charles Henry. Pensioner
(June 30, 1896); BA (1899); MA
(1903).

Sheepshanks, Arthur Charles.
Pensioner (25 June 1903); Class.
Trip. 2.1 (1906); Law Special, 2nd
(1906); BA (1906); MA (1920).

Wells, Robert Douglas. Pensioner (June
13, 1893); BA (1896); MA (1907).

West, Hercules Henry. Pensioner (May
25, 1875); Scholar (1876); Browne
Medal (1877); 1st; BA (7th Classic)
(1879); MA (1883).

TRINITY HALL
Wigram, Rev. William Ainger.
Admitted (1891); BA (1893).

D. Oxford Colleges

Balliol College

Clarke, Rupert Charles. Matriculated at Balliol College (15 October 1884); awarded a Stapeldon Scholarship at Exeter College (8 December 1884); Class. mods. 2nd (1886); Classics 2nd (1888); BA (25 October 1888); MA (28 April 1892).

Darbishire, Robert Shelby. Matriculated (1905); Modern History, 3rd; BA (1909).

Jones, Henry Stuart. Matriculated (1886); Hertford scholarship (1886); Class. mods. 1st (1888); Ireland and Cravan scholarships (1888); and Lit. Hum. 1st (1890).

Richards, George Chatterton, Class. mods. 1st (1887); Lit. Hum. 1st (1889); MA (1892).

Toynbee, Arnold Joseph. Matriculated (October 1907); Scholar; Class. mod.; Lit. Hum. (1911).

Brasenose College

Crowfoot, John Winter. Somerset Thornhill Manor Scholar (1892); Class. mod. 1st (1894); Lit. Hum. 2nd (1896); Senior Hulme Scholarship of Brasenose College (Lent, 1896); BA (1896); Hon. D. Litt. (1958).

Frost, Kingdon Tregosse. Admitted as Classics Exhibitioner to Lincoln

College, Oxford (1896); Junior
Hume Exhibitioner at Brasenose
College (Lent Term, 1897); Class.
mod. 2nd (1898); Lit. Hum. 3rd (1900);
BA (1900); MA (1905); BLitt,
'Studies in Greek athletic art;
Appendix: British Museum notes'
(1909).

CHRIST CHURCH

Anderson, John George Clark.
Exhibitioner (1891-96); Lit. Hum. 1st;
MA 1899.

Calder, William Moir. Exhibitioner
(1903); Scholar (1906); Class. mod.
1st (1905); Lit. Hum. (1907); BA
(1907).

Cheetham, J. Milne (Sir). Matriculated
(12 October 1888) as Scholar; 2nd
(1892).

Robinson, Edward Stanley Gotch.
Scholar (1906); Class. mod. 1st; BA
(1910); MA (1928); hon. D.Litt.
(1955).

CORPUS CHRISTI COLLEGE

Caspari, Max Otto Bismark (Max
Cary). Scholar; Class. mod. 1st
(1901); Lit. Hum. 1st (1903); D.Litt.
(1922).

Milne, Joseph Grafton. Scholar; Class.
mod. 1st (1888); Lit. Hum. 2nd (1890);
BA (1890); MA (1896); D.Litt. (1925).

Thompson, Maurice Scott. Class. mod.
3rd (1905), Lit. Hum. 2nd (1907); MA
(1912).

EXETER COLLEGE

Clarke, Rupert Charles. Matriculated at
Balliol College (15 October 1884);
awarded a Stapeldon Scholarship at
Exeter College (8 December 1884);
Class. mod. 2nd (1886); Lit. Hum. 2nd
(1888); BA (25 October 1888); MA
(28 April 1892).

Munro, John Arthur Ruskin. Class.
mod. 1st (1883); Lit. Hum. 1st (1886).

HERTFORD COLLEGE

Whatley, Norman. Class. mod. 1st; Lit.
Hum. 1st.

KEBLE COLLEGE

Penoyre, John ff. Baker.

LINCOLN COLLEGE

Casson, Stanley. Matric. (1908); Lit.
Hum. 2nd (1912); MA 1919.

Frost, Kingdon Tregosse. Admitted as
Classics Exhibitioner to Lincoln
College (1896); Junior Hume
Exhibitioner at Brasenose College
(Lent Term, 1897); Class. mod.
(1898); Lit. Hum. 3rd (1900); BA
(1900); MA (1905); BLitt, 'Studies in
Greek athletic art; Appendix:
British Museum notes' (1909).

MAGDALEN COLLEGE

Hoare, Edward Barclay. Commoner (1890-94); BA (1894).

Hogarth, David George. Commoner (1876-81); Class. mod. 1st (1882); Lit. Hum. 1st (1885).

Inge, Charles Cuthbert. Demy (1887-92); Class. mod. 1st (1889); Lit. Hum. 2nd; BA (1891); MA (1893).

Parry, Oswald Hutton. Exhibitioner (1887-91); Class. mod. 2nd (1889), Lit. Hum. 3rd (1891); BA (1891); MA (1895).

Piddington, John George (J.G. Smith). Commoner (1888-92); Class. mod. 2nd (1890); Lit. Hum. 3rd (1892); BA (1892).

Pirie-Gordon, Charles Harry Clinton, of Buthlaw. Commoner (1902-05); Modern History, 3rd; BA (1905); MA (1909).

Stainer, John Frederick Randall. Exhibitioner (1885-89); Class. mod. 1st (1887); Lit. Hum. 2nd (1889); BA (1889); MA; BCL (1892).

Welch, Francis Bertram. Exhibitioner (1894-98); Class. mod. 2nd (1896); Lit. Hum. 1st (1898); BA (1898); MA (1902).

Woodward, Arthur Maurice. Demy (1902-6); Class. mod. 2nd (1904); Lit. Hum. 2nd (1906); BA (1906), MA (1909).

MERTON COLLEGE
Fotheringham, John Knight.
Exhibitioner; Lit. Hum. 1st (1896);
History, 1st (1897).

NEW COLLEGE
Awdry, Herbert. Winchester Scholar
(14 Oct 1870); Lit. Hum. 2nd (1874);
MA (1877).

Bevan, Edwyn Robert. Open classical
scholarship; Class. mod. 1st (1890);
Lit. Hum. 1st (1892).

Brown, Alexander Cradock Bolney.
Winchester Scholar (11 October
1901); Class. mod. 1st (1903); Lit.
Hum. 2nd (1905); BA (1905); MA
(1909).

Cheesman, George Leonard.
Winchester Scholar (October 1903);
Class. mod. 1st (1905); Lit. Hum. 1st
(1907); BA (1907); MA (1910).

Dickins, Guy. Scholar (1900); Class.
mod. 2nd (1902), Lit. Hum. 1st (1904);
MA (1907).

Halliday (Hoffmeister), William
Reginald. Winchester Scholar
(October 1905); Lit. Hum. 1st (1909);
MA (1928).

Moss-Blundell, Cyril Bertram. Scholar
(1910); Class. mod. 1st (1912); Lit.
Hum. 1st; BA (1914). Specialised in
Classical Archaeology.

Myres, John Linton. Scholar; Class.
mod. 1st (1890); Lit. Hum. 1st (1892).

Oppé, Adolph Paul. New College. Exhibitioner; Class. mod. 1st (1899); Lit. Hum. 1st (1901).

ORIEL COLLEGE

Edgar, Campbell Cowan. Admitted as Bible Clerk (1891); Class. mod. 1st (1893); Lit. Hum. 1st (1895); BA (1897).

Forster, Edward Seymour. Bishop Frazer's Scholar; Class. mod. 1st (1900); Lit. Hum. 2nd (1902); BA (1903); MA (1905).

Heath, Roger Meyrick. Scholar, (1908); Class. mod. 1st (1910); Lit. Hum. 1st (1912); BA (1912); Bishop Fraser Scholar (1912); Diploma in Classical Archaeology, distinction.

PEMBROKE COLLEGE

Tubbs, H. Arnold. Matriculated (1883), aged 18; scholar (1883-87); BA (1887).

THE QUEEN'S COLLEGE

Ormerod, Henry Arderne. Scholar; Class. mod. 2nd (1907); Lit. Hum. 1st (1909).

Peet, Thomas Eric. Scholar; Class. mod. (1903); Lit. Hum. 2nd (1905).

Spilsbury, Alfred John. Jodrell Scholar (reserved for those studying Divinity, Classics, or Mathematics); Class. mod. 1st (1895); Lit. Hum. 2nd (1897).

Woodhouse, William John. Class. mod.
1st; Lit. Hum. 1st; BA (1889).

ST JOHN'S COLLEGE
Tod, Marcus Niebuhr. Class. mod. 1st
(1897); Lit. Hum. (1901); MA (1905).

UNIVERSITY COLLEGE
Hopkinson, John Henry. Matriculated
(Michaelmas 1895); Scholar (1895);
Class. mod. 1st (1897); Lit. Hum. 2nd
(1899); BA (1899); MA (1902).

WADHAM COLLEGE
Lambert, Richard Stanton. Classical
Scholar (1912); B.A. (1918).
Webster, Erwin Wentworth. Scholar
(1898); Class. mod. 1st; Taylorian
Scholar in German, (1901); Lit.
Hum. 1st (1902).

E. Universities and Educational Establishments in England

Liverpool School of Architecture

Budden, Lionel Bailey. Liverpool School of Architecture (1905); BA (1909); MA (1910).

London University

Bickford-Smith, Roandeu Albert Henry. University of London, honours in Mathematics (1876).

King's College London

Conway, Agnes Ethel (Hon. Mrs Horsfall). King's College, London, MA.

Dawkins, Richard Mcgillivray. King's College London (1890-92), Electrical Engineering.

Royal Holloway College

Rosenörn-Lehn, Baroness E.

University College London

Abrahams, Ethel Beatrice (Mrs Culley).

Atkinson, Thomas Dinham.

Doll, Christian Charles Tyler. Architectural Diploma, University College, London (1903).

Rosenörn-Lehn, Baroness E.

Smith, Ravenscroft Elsey. Slade School, University College London (1877-78).

F. Universities and Educational Establishments in Scotland

Aberdeen, King's College
Findlay, Adam Fyfe.

Aberdeen University
Anderson, John George Clark.
Calder, William Moir. Classics, 1st (1903).
Hardie, Margaret Masson (Mrs F.W. Hasluck). Classics, 1st.
Reid, W.W.

Dundee, University College
Lorimer, (Elizabeth) Hilda Lockhart. (1889-93); BA 1st.

Edinburgh University
Curtis, William Alexander. Heriot Scholar. D.Litt., D.D. (Edin.)
Hamilton, John Arnott. Holder of the Blackie Scholarship.
Mackenzie, Duncan. Arts Faculty (1882-90); MA in Philosophy.
Paterson, Archibald. MA, Classical Literature, 2nd (1888).
Reid, W.W.

Glasgow School of Art
Fyfe, David Theodore. Architectural training (1890-91, 1894-95, 1895-96, 1896-97).

Orr, Frank George. Architecture and
Modelling (1898-1901, 1902-03).

GLASGOW UNIVERSITY

Edgar, Campbell Cowan. (1887-91);
MA (1897).
Frazer, James George. (1869-74). MA
(1874).

ST ANDREWS

Hamilton, Mary (Mrs G. Dickins).

G. University and Educational Establishments in Ireland

Trinity College, Dublin
Boxwell, J. Scholar.

H. UNIVERSITIES AND EDUCATIONAL ESTABLISHMENTS OUTSIDE GREAT BRITAIN

UNIVERSITY COLLEGE, TORONTO
Kirkwood, William Alexander.

VICTORIA COLLEGE, UNIVERSITY OF TORONTO
Currelly, Charles Trick. BA (1898); MA (1902).

UNIVERSITY OF VIENNA
Mackenzie, Duncan. Doctorate (1895).

I. FELLOWSHIPS AT CAMBRIDGE COLLEGES

CHRIST'S COLLEGE
Grose, Sidney Wilson. Fellow 1919 and Senior Tutor 1922; Praelector; Librarian; Vice-Master.

EMMANUEL COLLEGE
Dawkins, Richard Mcgillivray. Fellow 1904; Hon. Fellow 1922.

GONVILLE & CAIUS COLLEGE
Gardner, Ernest Arthur. Fellow 1885-94.

JESUS COLLEGE
Duckworth, Wynfrid Laurence Henry. Fellow 1893; Steward 1895-1920 and 1929; Bursar 1933; Master 1940-. Senior Proctor 1904. University Lecturer in Physical Anthropology (1898-1920); Additional Demonstrator of Human Anatomy (1898-1907); Senior Demonstrator of Anatomy (1907-20); Reader in Human Anatomy (1920-40).

Farrell, Wilfrid Jerome. Fellow (short-term) 1906.

Laistner, Max Ludwig Wolfram. Hon. Fellow 1949.

Tillyard, Eustace Mandeville Wetenhall. Prize Fellowship 1912-14, working on the Hope Vases;

Fellow 1913-15, 1934-45, 1959-62;
Director of Studies in English 1934;
Senior Tutor 1941; University
Lecturer in English 1926-54; Master
of Jesus College 1945-59.

KING'S COLLEGE

Bather, Arthur George. Fellow 1894.
Earp, Frank (Francis) Russell. Fellow
1897.
Hasluck, Frederick William. Fellow
1904.
James, Montague Rhodes. Fellow 1887-
1905; Dean and Tutor; Provost
1905-18; Hon. Fellow 1918.
Loring, William. Fellow 1891-97.
Marshall, John Hubert. Hon. Fellow
1927.
Mayor, Robert John Grote. Fellow
1894.
Yorke, Vincent Wodehouse. Fellow
1895.

MAGDALENE COLLEGE

Benson, Edward Frederic. Hon. Fellow
1938.

PEMBROKE COLLEGE

Lawson, John Cuthbert. Fellow 1899-
1935; Tutor and Classical Lecturer;
Junior Proctor 1909; Senior Proctor
1912.
Wace, Alan John Bayard. Fellow, 1904-
13, 1934-44; Laurence Professor of
Classical Archaeology at

Cambridge, 1934-44; Hon. Fellow
1951.

St John's College
Sikes, Edward Ernest. Fellow 1891-
1940; Tutor 1900-25; President 1925-
37.

Trinity College
Frazer, James George. Fellow 1879.

J. Fellowships at Oxford Colleges

Balliol College
Jones, Henry Stuart. Hon. Fellow 1936.
Toynbee, Arnold Joseph. Fellow and Tutor 1912.

Brasenose College
Anderson, John George Clark. Fellow 1927-36; Reader in Roman Epigraphy; Camden Professor of Ancient History.
Jones, Henry Stuart. Fellow 1919; Camden Professor of Ancient History; Hon. Fellow 1928.

Christ Church
Anderson, John George Clark. Student and Tutor 1900-27; University Lecturer 1919-27.
Myres, John Linton. Fellow 1892-94. Student and Tutor of Christ Church 1895-1907; University Lecturer in Classical Archaeology; Junior Proctor (1904-05).

Exeter College
Dawkins, Richard Mcgillivray. Fellow 1922; Hon. Fellow 1939. Professor of Byzantine and Modern Greek 1920-39
Munro, John Arthur Ruskin. Hon. Fellow 1929.

HERTFORD COLLEGE

Richards, George Chatterton. Fellow 1889.

Whatley, Norman. Fellow 1907-23; Tutor and Lecturer 1908-23; Dean 1912-1920.

LINCOLN COLLEGE

Anderson, John George Clark. Fellow; Hon. Fellow 1936.

Munro, John Arthur Ruskin. Fellow 1888; Bursar 1904-19; Rector 1919.

MAGDALEN COLLEGE

Fotheringham, John Knight. Senior Demy 1898-1902; Research Fellow 1909-16.

Hogarth, David G. Fellow and Tutor 1886-93.

Myres, John Linton. Fellow 1892-94.

NEW COLLEGE

Casson, Stanley. Fellow 1920.

Cheesman, George Leonard. Fellow 1908.

Halliday (Hoffmeister), William Reginald. Fellow 1912.

Myres, John Linton. Wykeham Professor of Ancient History and Fellow of New College 1910-1939.

ORIEL COLLEGE

Richards, George Chatterton. Fellow
and Tutor 1899-1927; Senior Proctor
1907.

Tod, Marcus Niebuhr. Fellow 1903;
Librarian; Senior Tutor; Vice-
Provost 1934-45; Hon. Fellow 1947.
University Lecturer in Greek
Epigraphy 1907; Reader 1927.

ST JOHN'S COLLEGE

Brown, Alexander Cradock Bolney.
Fereday Fellow 1908-15.

Dickins, Guy. Fellow 1909. University
Lecturer in Classical Archaeology
1914.

Tod, Marcus Niebuhr. Hon. Fellow
1946.

SOMERVILLE COLLEGE

Lorimer, (Elizabeth) Hilda Lockhart.
Classical Tutor 1896-1934; Tutor in
Classical Archaeology 1934-1939;
Hon. Fellow 1939.

TRINITY COLLEGE

Jones, Henry Stuart. Non-official
Fellowship 1890-93; Fellow 1894;
Tutor 1896; Research Fellowship
1903 (as Director of the British
School at Rome); Hon. Fellow 1935.

WADHAM COLLEGE

Webster, Erwin Wentworth. Fellow
1903; Tutor 1913.

K. STUDENTS BY YEAR OF ADMISSION AT THE BSA

F.C. PENROSE (1886-1887)

Gardner, Ernest Arthur. Gonville & Caius, Cambridge. Admitted 1886/87 (Cambridge and Craven University Student).

Hogarth, David George. Magdalen, Oxford. Craven University Fellow (1886). Admitted 1886/87; re-admitted 1887/88 (for work on Cyprus).

Clarke, Rupert Charles. Exeter, Oxford. Admitted 1886/87.

E.A. GARDNER (1887-95)

Guillemard, Francis Henry Hill. Gonville & Caius, Cambridge. Admitted 1887/88 (for work in Cyprus).

James, Montague Rhodes. King's, Cambridge. Admitted 1887/88 (for work in Cyprus, with a grant of £100 from Cambridge University). Engaged in digging in Cyprus with Dr Hogarth and Dr Ernest Gardner, mainly at Paphos (1887).

Smith, Ravenscroft Elsey. RIBA Studentship, 1887/88.

Schultz Weir, Robert Weir (R.W. Schultz). BSA, Gold Medallist and Travelling Student in Architecture of the Royal Academy of Arts,

1887/88; re-admitted 1888/89,
1889/90.

Barnsley, Sidney Howard. Admitted as
Student of the Royal Academy,
1887/88; re-admitted 1889/90,
1890/91.

Munro, John Arthur Ruskin. Fellow of
Lincoln, Oxford. Admitted 1888/89
(for work on Cyprus); re-admitted
1889/90 (Cyprus).

Tubbs, H. Arnold. Pembroke, Oxford.
Craven University Fellow.
Admitted 1888/89 (for work on
Cyprus); re-admitted (Cyprus)
1889/90.

Frazer, James George. Fellow of
Trinity, Cambridge. Admitted
1889/90.

Loring, William. King's, Cambridge.
Admitted 1889/90 (Cambridge
Studentship); re-admitted 1890/91
(Craven University Student),
1891/92, 1892/93.

Woodhouse, William John. Queen's,
Oxford. Admitted 1889/90
(Appointed to Oxford Studentship;
Sir Charles Newton Studentship);
re-admitted 1891/92, 1892/93
(Craven University Fellow).

Richards, George Chatterton. Fellow of
Hertford, Oxford. Admitted
1889/90 (Craven University
Fellow); re-admitted 1890/91.

Parry, Oswald Hutton. Magdalen,
Oxford. Admitted 1889/90.

Stainer, John Frederick Randall.
Magdalen, Oxford. Admitted
1889/90.
Bickford-Smith, Roandeu Albert
Henry. Trinity, Cambridge.
Admitted 1889/90.
Bather, Arthur George. King's,
Cambridge. Admitted 1889/90; re-
admitted 1891/92 (Cambridge
Studentship); 1892/93 (Prendergast
Greek Student); 1893/94
(Cambridge Student).
Sikes, Edward Ernest. St John's,
Cambridge. Admitted 1890/91
(Cambridge Studentship).
Milne, Joseph Grafton. Corpus Christi,
Oxford. Admitted 1890/91 (Oxford
Studentship).
Jones, Henry Stuart. Fellow of Trinity,
Oxford. Admitted 1890/91 (Craven
University Fellow); re-admitted
1892/93.
Sellers, Eugénie (Mrs A. Arthur
Strong). Girton, Cambridge.
Admitted 1890/91.
Baker, Francis Brayne (Brayne-Baker).
Christ's, Cambridge. Admitted
1891/92.
Inge, Charles Cuthbert. Magdalen,
Oxford. Admitted 1891/92 (Oxford
Studentship)
Benson, Edward Frederic. King's,
Cambridge. Admitted 1891/92
(with grant of £100 from the Worts
Fund); 1892/93 (Cambridge

Studentship); 1893/94 (Craven Student); 1894/95 (Prendergast Student).

Piddington, John George (J.G. Smith). Magdalen, Oxford. Admitted 1891/92; re-admitted 1895/96 as assistant to the Director.

Yorke, Vincent Wodehouse. King's, Cambridge. Admitted 1892/93; re-admitted 1893/94.

Myres, John Linton. Fellow of Magalen, Oxford. Admitted 1892/93 (Craven Fellow); re-admitted 1893/94, 1894/95. Hon. Student of the School.

Mayor, Robert John Grote. King's, Cambridge. Admitted 1892/93.

Bosanquet, Robert Carr. Trinity, Cambridge. Admitted 1892/93; re-admitted 1894/95 (Craven University Student); 1895/96, 1896/97 (Craven Student).

Cheetham, J. Milne (Sir). Christ Church, Oxford. Admitted 1892/93 (Oxford Studentship).

Bevan, Edwyn Robert. New, Oxford. Admitted 1893/94.

Findlay, Adam Fyfe. United Presbyterian Church. Admitted 1894/95.

Duncan, John Garrow. Church of Scotland. Admitted 1894/95.

Brooks, John Ellingham. Peterhouse, Cambridge, Admitted 1894/95; re-admitted as associate 1896/97.

Awdry, Herbert. New, Oxford.
Admitted 1894/95.

C. HARCOURT-SMITH (C. SMITH) (1895-97)

Mackenzie, Duncan. University of
Vienna. Admitted 1895/96; re-
admitted 1896/97, 1897/98,
1898/99.

Paterson, Archibald. Edinburgh. BSA,
1895/96.

Clark, Charles Richmond Rowland.
Admitted 1895/96; re-admitted
1896/97, by the Managing
Committee to an Architectural
Studentship.

Edgar, Campbell Cowan. Oriel,
Oxford. Admitted 1895/96; re-
admitted 1896/97 (Craven
University Fellow), 1897/98,
1898/99.

Earp, Frank (Francis) Russell. King's,
Cambridge. Admitted 1896/97.

Morrison, Frederick Arthur Charles.
Jesus, Cambridge. Admitted
1896/97 (Prendergast Student).

West, Hercules Henry. Trinity,
Cambridge. Admitted 1896/97.

Hutton, Caroline Amy. Girton,
Cambridge. Admitted 1896/97.

Rodeck, Pieter. Admitted 1896/97
(Travelling Student and Gold
Medallist of the Royal Academy).

Anderson, John George Clark. Christ Church, Oxford. Admitted 1896/97 (Craven University Fellow)

D.G. HOGARTH (1897-1900)

Crowfoot, John Winter. Brasenose, Oxford. Admitted 1896/97 (Oxford Studentship); re-admitted 1897/98.

Reid, W.W. Aberdeen and Edinburgh. Admitted as holder of Blackie Travelling Studentship, 1896/97.

Henderson, Arthur Edward. Admitted 1897/98 (Owen Jones Student of Royal Institute of British Architects); re-admitted 1898/99, 1901/02 and 1902/03.

Curtis, William Alexander. Edinburgh. Admitted 1897/98.

Spilsbury, Alfred John. Queen's, Oxford. Admitted 1897/98 (Oxford Studentship).

Hoare, Edward Barclay. Magdalen, Oxford. Admitted 1897/98 (Architectural Student)

Lawson, John Cuthbert. Pembroke, Cambridge. Admitted 1898/99 (Craven University Student); re-admitted 1899/1900.

Edmonds, Charles Douglas. Emmanuel, Cambridge. Admitted 1898/99 (Prendergast Student).

Marshall, John Hubert. King's, Cambridge. Admitted 1898/99; re-admitted 1900/01 (Prendergast

Student), 1901/02 (Craven
Student).

Gutch, Clement. King's, Cambridge.
Admitted 1898/99 (Cambridge
Studentship).

Welch, Francis Bertram. Magdalen,
Oxford. Admitted 1898/99 (Craven
University Fellow); re-admitted
1899/1900.

Atkinson, Thomas Dinham. Admitted
as Architectural Student, 1898/99.

Fotheringham, John Knight. Senior
Demy at Magdalen, Oxford.
Admitted 1898/99 (Oxford
Studentship).

Hopkinson, John Henry. University,
Oxford. Admitted 1899/1900,
1900/01 (Craven University
Fellow).

Smith, Solomon Charles Kaines.
Magdalene, Cambridge. Admitted
1899/1900 (Cambridge
Studentship).

Kohler, O.C. (Mrs Charles Smith).
Girton, Cambridge. Admitted
1899/1900.

Fyfe, David Theodore. Glasgow School
of Art. Admitted 1899/1900, on
appointment to Architectural
Studentship.

R.C. BOSANQUET (1900-06)

Frost, Kingdon Tregosse. Brasenose,
Oxford. Admitted 1900/01 (Oxford
Studentship).

Wells, Robert Douglas. Trinity, Cambridge. Admitted 1900/01 (Architectural Studentship).

Penoyre, John ff. Baker. Keble, Oxford. Admitted 1900/01; re-admitted 1906/07, 1907/08.

Tod, Marcus Niebuhr. St John's, Oxford. Admitted 1901/02 (Senior Studentship). Assistant Director, 1902/04.

Hasluck, Frederick William. King's Cambridge. Admitted 1901/02 (Cambridge Studentship); re-admitted 1902/03, 1904/05, 1905/06. Assistant Director and Librarian, 1906/15.

Comyn, Charles Heaton Fitzwilliam. Admitted on appointment to the Architectural Studentship, 1901/02; re-admitted 1903/04.

Lorimer, (Elizabeth) Hilda Lockhart. Classical Tutor of Somerville College, Oxford. Admitted as Pfeiffer Travelling Student 1901/02.

Rosenörn-Lehn, Baroness E. Royal Holloway College, and University College London. Admitted 1901/02.

Oppé, Adolph Paul. New, Oxford. Admitted 1901/02.

Duckworth, Wynfrid Laurence Henry. Fellow of Jesus, Cambridge. Admitted 1902/03.

Currelly, Charles Trick. Victoria College, Toronto. Admitted 1902/03; re-admitted 1903/04.

Dawkins, Richard Mcgillivray. Emmanuel, Cambridge. Admitted 1902/03; re-admitted 1903/04 (Craven Student); re-admitted 1904/05. Director, 1906/13.

Forster, Edward Seymour. Oriel, Oxford. Admitted 1902/03 (Oxford Studentship); re-admitted 1903/04 (with grants from the Craven Fund and Oriel College).

Wace, Alan John Bayard. Pembroke, Cambridge. Admitted 1902/03; re-admitted 1903/04, 1904/05, 1905/06, 1906/07, 1907/08, 1908/09, 1909/10, 1910/11. Hon. Student of the School. Director of the School 1914-23.

Webster, Erwin Wentworth. Wadham, Oxford. Admitted 1902/03. In the same year he studied in Berlin for a term and travelled in Italy.

Fulton, James Black. Admitted 1902/03. Soane Student.

Reynolds, Edwin Francis. Admitted 1902/03.

Caspari, Max Otto Bismark (Max Cary). Corpus Christi, Oxford. Admitted 1903/04. School Student.

Stokes, John Laurence. Pembroke, Cambridge. Admitted 1903-/04 (as holder of the Prior Scholarship from Pembroke College).

Welsh, Margery Katharine (Mrs A. M. Daniel). Newnham, Cambridge. Admitted 1903-04.

Dickins, Guy. New, Oxford. Craven University Fellow (1904). Admitted 1904/05; re-admitted 1905/06, 1906/07 (School Student), 1907/08, 1908/09; re-admitted 1912/13.

Doll, Christian Charles Tyler. Trinity, Cambridge; University College London. Admitted 1904/05.

Hawes, Charles Henry. Trinity, Cambridge. Admitted 1904/05.

Kirkwood, William Alexander. University College, Toronto. Admitted 1904/05.

Tillyard, Henry Julius Wetenhall. Gonville & Caius, Cambridge. BSA, 1904-/05 (Assistant Librarian); re-admitted 1905/06 (Studentship), 1906/07, 1908/09; re-admitted 1912/13.

Richter, Gisela Marie Augusta. Girton, Cambridge. Admitted 1904/05.

Droop, John Percival. Trinity, Cambridge. Admitted 1905/06; re-admitted 1906/07 (Prendergast Student), 1907/08, 1908/09, 1910/11; re-admitted 1912/13, 1913/14.

Hamilton, Mary (Mrs G. Dickins). St Andrews. Admitted 1905/06, 1906/07.

Brown, Alexander Cradock Bolney. New, Oxford. Admitted 1905/06.

Orr, Frank George. Glasgow School of Art. Admitted 1905/06.

Traquair, Ramsay. Admitted 1905/06, on appointment to an architectural studentship.

Abrahams, Ethel Beatrice (Mrs Culley). University College London. Admitted 1905/06.

R.M. DAWKINS (1906-14)

Farrell, Wilfrid Jerome. Jesus, Cambridge. Admitted 1906/07; re-admitted 1907/08, 1908/09.

George, Walter Sykes. Admitted 1906/07; re-admitted 1908/09, 1909/10, as Student of the Byzantine Research Fund; re-admitted 1912/13.

Peet, Thomas Eric. Queen's, Oxford. Admitted 1906/07 (Craven Fellow), 1908/09.

Woodward, Arthur Maurice. Magdalen, Oxford. Admitted 1906/07, 1907/08, 1908/09. Assistant Director, 1909/10.

Calder, William Moir. Christ Church, Oxford. Craven Fellowship 1907. Admitted 1907/08.

Harvey, W. Admitted 1907/08. Gold Medallist and Travelling Student of the Royal Academy.

Pirie-Gordon, Charles Harry Clinton, of Buthlaw. Magdalen, Oxford. Admitted 1907/08.

Thompson, Maurice Scott. Corpus Christi, Oxford. Admitted 1907/08 (Holder of Charles Oldham University Scholarship), 1908/09, 1909/10 (1908-10, Craven Fellowship), 1910/11.

Sheepshanks, Arthur Charles. Trinity, Cambridge. Admitted 1907/08.

Whatley, Norman. Fellow of Hertford College, Oxford. Admitted 1907/08.

Cheesman, George Leonard. Fellow of New College, Oxford. Admitted 1908/09.

Gomme, Arnold Wycombe. Trinity, Cambridge. Admitted 1908/09 (Prendergast Student).

Budden, Lionel Bailey. Liverpool School of Architecture. Admitted 1909/10.

Grose, Sidney Wilson. Christ's, Cambridge. Admitted 1909/10 (School Student).

Ormerod, Henry Arderne. Queen's, Oxford. Admitted 1909/10, 1910/11.

Jewell, Harry Herbert. Admitted 1909/10. Royal Academy Gold Medallist.

Halliday (Hoffmeister), William Reginald. New, Oxford. Admitted 1910/11; re-admitted 1912/13.

Lamb, Dorothy (Mrs J. Reeve Brooke). Newnham, Cambridge. Admitted 1910/11; re-admitted 1913/14.

Tennant, Lilian Elizabeth (Mrs F.J.
Watson-Taylor). Admitted 1910/11.

Robinson, Edward Stanley Gotch.
Christ Church, Oxford. Admitted
1910-11 (School Student); Craven
studentship.

Tillard, Laurence Berkley. St John's,
Cambridge. Admitted 1910/11.

Toynbee, Arnold Joseph. Balliol,
Oxford. Admitted 1911/12.

Darbishire, Robert Shelby. Balliol,
Oxford. Admitted 1911/12.

Hardie, Margaret Masson (Mrs F.W.
Hasluck). Newnham, Cambridge.
Admitted 1911/12 (school student).

Tillyard, Eustace Mandeville
Wetenhall. Jesus, Cambridge.
Craven Student. Admitted 1911/12.

Laistner, Max Ludwig Wolfram. Jesus,
Cambridge. Craven Student (1912).
Admitted 1912/13; re-admitted
1913/14 (School Student).

Casson, Stanley. Senior Scholar of St
John's College, Oxford. Admitted
1912/13 (School Student), re-
admitted 1913/14.

Lambert, Richard Stanton.
Subsequently Wadham, Oxford.
Admitted 1912/13.

Leith, George Esslemont Gordon.
Admitted 1912/13. Herbert Baker
Studentship.

Scutt, Cecil Allison. Clare, Cambridge.
Admitted 1912/13 (Prendergast
Student); re-admitted 1913/14.

Heath, Roger Meyrick. Oriel, Oxford.
Admitted 1913/14.
Boxwell, J. Trinity College Dublin.
Admitted 1913/14.
Taylor, Mary Norah Luton (Mrs
M.N.L. Bradshaw). Newnham,
Cambridge. Admitted 1913/14.
Hamilton, John Arnott. Edinburgh.
Holder of the Blackie Scholarship.
Admitted 1913/14.
Radford, Evelyn. Newnham,
Cambridge. Admitted 1913/14.
Conway, Agnes Ethel (Hon. Mrs
Horsfall). Newnham, Cambridge.
Admitted 1913/14.
Wigram, Rev. William Ainger. Trinity
Hall, Cambridge. Admitted
1913/14.

A.J.B. WACE (1914-23)

Moss-Blundell, Cyril Bertram. New,
Oxford. Student elect 1914/15.
[Commissioned in the Durham
Light Infantry, January 1915.]

L. DIRECTORS AND STUDENTS LISTED IN THE OXFORD DICTIONARY OF NATIONAL BIOGRAPHY (2004)

1. DIRECTORS

'Penrose, Francis Cranmer (1817–1903)',
by Paul Waterhouse, revised by
Roderick O'Donnell.

'Gardner, Ernest Arthur (1862–1939)', by J.
M. C. Toynbee and H. D. A. Major,
revised by David Gill.

'Smith, Sir Cecil Harcourt- (1859–1944)',
by James Laver, revised by Dennis
Farr.

'Hogarth, David George (1862–1927)', by
David Gill.

'Bosanquet, Robert Carr (1871–1935)', by
E. S. Bosanquet, revised by David Gill.

'Dawkins, Richard MacGillivray (1871–
1955)', by W. R. Halliday, revised by
David Gill.

'Wace, Alan John Bayard (1879–1957)', by
David Gill.

2. STUDENTS

'Barnsley family (per. 1885–1987)', by Alan Crawford.

'Benson, Edward Frederic (1867–1940)', by Sayoni Basu.

'Bevan, Edwyn Robert (1870–1943)', by Gilbert Murray and Clement C. J. Webb, revised by Michael H. Crawford.

'Duckworth, Wynfrid Laurence Henry (1870–1956)', by J. D. Boyd, revised.

'Fotheringham, John Knight (1874–1936)', by F. R. Stephenson.

'Frazer, Sir James George (1854–1941)', by Robert Ackerman.

'Hasluck, Frederick William (1878–1920)', by Peter W. Lock.

'Hasluck, Margaret Masson (1885–1948)', by Roderick Bailey.

'James, Montague Rhodes (1862–1936)', by Richard W. Pfaff.

'Jones, Sir Henry Stuart- (1867–1939)', by H. E. D. Blakiston, revised by David Gill.

'Lorimer, (Elizabeth) Hilda Lockhart (1873–1954)', by Helen Waterhouse.

'Mackenzie, Duncan (1861–1934)', by Nicoletta Momigliano.

'Marshall, Sir John Hubert (1876–1958)', by Mortimer Wheeler, revised by Jane McIntosh.

'Myres, Sir John Linton (1869–1954)', by John Boardman, revised.

'Oppé, Adolph Paul (1878–1957)', by
   Brinsley Ford, revised.
'Peet, (Thomas) Eric (1882–1934)', by,
   Battiscombe Gunn, revised by R. S.
   Simpson.
'Robinson, Sir (Edward) Stanley Gotch
   (1887–1976)', by N. J. Mayhew.
'Strong , Eugénie (1860–1943)', by J. M. C.
   Toynbee, revised by Stephen L. Dyson.
'Tod, Marcus Niebuhr (1878–1974)', by
   Michael H. Crawford.
'Toynbee, Arnold Joseph (1889–1975)', by
   Fergus Millar.
'Wigram, William Ainger (1872–1953)', by
   J. F. Coakley.

M. Alphabetical List of Students

Abrahams, Ethel Beatrice (b. 1881) (Mrs Culley). University College London.

Anderson, John George Clark (1870-1952). Christ Church, Oxford.

Atkinson, Thomas Dinham (1864-1948). Architectural Student.

Awdry, Herbert (1851-1909). New, Oxford.

Baker, Francis Brayne (Brayne-Baker) (b. 1868). Christ's, Cambridge.

Barnsley, Sidney Howard (1865-1926). Student of the Royal Academy.

Bather, Arthur George (1868-1928). King's, Cambridge.

Benson, Edward Frederic (1867-1940). King's, Cambridge.

Bevan, Edwyn Robert (1870-1943). New, Oxford.

Bickford-Smith, Roandeu Albert Henry (1859-1916). Trinity, Cambridge.

Bosanquet, Robert Carr (1871-1935). Trinity, Cambridge.

Boxwell, J. Trinity College Dublin.

Bradshaw, Mary N.L. *See Taylor, Mary N.L.*

Brayne-Baker, Francis. *See Baker, Francis Brayne.*

Brooke, Dorothy. *See Lamb, Dorothy.*

Brooks, John Ellingham (1863-1929). Peterhouse, Cambridge.

Brown, Alexander Cradock Bolney (1882-1942). New, Oxford.

Budden, Lionel Bailey (1887-1956).
Liverpool School of Architecture.
Calder, William Moir (1881-1960). Christ
Church, Oxford.
Cary, Max. *See Caspari, Max Otto Bismark.*
Caspari, Max Otto Bismark (Max Cary)
(1881-1958). Corpus Christi, Oxford.
Casson, Stanley (1889-1944). Senior
Scholar of St John's College, Oxford.
Cheesman, George Leonard (1884-1915).
Fellow of New College, Oxford.
Cheetham, J. Milne (Sir) (1869-1938).
Christ Church, Oxford.
Clark, Charles Richmond Rowland (1869-
1933). Architectural Studentship.
Clarke, Rupert Charles (1866-1912). Exeter,
Oxford.
Comyn, Charles Heaton Fitzwilliam (1877-
1933). Architectural Studentship.
Conway, Agnes Ethel (Hon. Mrs Horsfall)
(1885-1950). Newnham, Cambridge.
Crowfoot, John Winter (1873-1959).
Brasenose, Oxford.
Currelly, Charles Trick (1876-1957).
Victoria College, Toronto.
Curtis, William Alexander (b. 1876).
Edinburgh.
Daniel, Margery Katharine. *See Welsh,
Margery Katharine.*
Darbishire, Robert Shelby (1886-1949).
Balliol, Oxford.
Dawkins, Richard Mcgillivray (1871-1955).
Emmanuel, Cambridge.
Dickins, Guy (1881-1916). New, Oxford.

Doll, Christian Charles Tyler (b. 1880). Trinity, Cambridge; University College London.

Droop, John Percival (1882-1963). Trinity, Cambridge.

Duckworth, Wynfrid Laurence Henry (1870-1956). Fellow of Jesus, Cambridge.

Duncan, John Garrow. Church of Scotland.

Earp, Frank (Francis) Russell (1871-1955). King's, Cambridge.

Edgar, Campbell Cowan (1870-1938). Oriel, Oxford.

Edmonds, Charles Douglas (b. 1876). Emmanuel, Cambridge.

Farrell, Wilfrid Jerome (1882-1960). Jesus, Cambridge.

Findlay, Adam Fyfe (1869-1962). United Presbyterian Church.

Forster, Edward Seymour (1879-1950). Oriel, Oxford.

Fotheringham, John Knight (1874-1936). Senior Demy at Magdalen, Oxford.

Frazer, James George (1854-1941). Fellow of Trinity, Cambridge.

Frost, Kingdon Tregosse (1877-1914). Brasenose, Oxford.

Fulton, James Black (1876-1922). Soane Student.

Fyfe, David Theodore (1875-1945). Glasgow School of Art.

Gardner, Ernest Arthur (1862-1939). Gonville & Caius, Cambridge.

George, Walter Sykes (1881-1962). Student
of the Byzantine Research Fund.
Gomme, Arnold Wycombe (1886-1959).
Trinity, Cambridge.
Grose, Sidney Wilson (1886-1980).
Christ's, Cambridge.
Guillemard, Francis Henry Hill (1852-
1933). Gonville & Caius, Cambridge.
Gutch, Clement (1875-1908). King's,
Cambridge.
Halliday (Hoffmeister), William Reginald
(1886-1966). New, Oxford.
Hamilton, John Arnott. Edinburgh.
Hamilton, Mary (Mrs G. Dickins). St
Andrews.
Hardie, Margaret Masson (Mrs F.W.
Hasluck) (1885-1948). Newnham,
Cambridge.
Harvey, W. Travelling Student of the
Royal Academy.
Hasluck, Frederick William (1878-1920).
King's Cambridge.
Hasluck, Margaret Masson. *See Hardie,
Margaret Masson.*
Hawes, Charles Henry (1867-1943).
Trinity, Cambridge.
Heath, Roger Meyrick (1889-1916). Oriel,
Oxford.
Henderson, Arthur Edward (1870-1956).
Owen Jones Student of Royal Institute
of British Architects.
Hoare, Edward Barclay (1872-1943).
Magdalen, Oxford.
Hoffmeister, William Reginald. *See
Halliday, William Reginald.*

Hogarth, David George (1862-1927).
    Magdalen, Oxford.
Hopkinson, John Henry (1876-1957).
    University, Oxford.
Horsfall, Hon. Mrs. *See Conway, Agnes
    Ethel.*
Hutton, Caroline Amy (c. 1861-1931).
    Girton, Cambridge.
Inge, Charles Cuthbert (1868-1957).
    Magdalen, Oxford.
James, Montague Rhodes (1862-1936).
    King's, Cambridge.
Jewell, Harry Herbert (1882-1974). Royal
    Academy Gold Medallist.
Jones, Henry Stuart (1867-1939). Fellow of
    Trinity, Oxford.
Kaines-Smith, Solomon Charles. *See Smith,
    Solomon Charles Kaines.*
Kirkwood, William Alexander. University
    College, Toronto.
Kohler, O.C. (Mrs Charles Smith). Girton,
    Cambridge.
Laistner, Max Ludwig Wolfram (1890-
    1959). Jesus, Cambridge.
Lamb, Dorothy (Mrs J. Reeve Brooke)
    (1887-1967). Newnham, Cambridge.
Lambert, Richard Stanton (1894-1981).
    Subsequently Wadham, Oxford.
Lawson, John Cuthbert (1874-1935).
    Pembroke, Cambridge.
Leith, George Esslemont Gordon (1886-
    1965). Herbert Baker Studentship.
Lorimer, (Elizabeth) Hilda Lockhart (1873-
    1954). Classical tutor of Somerville
    College, Oxford.

Loring, William (1865-1915). King's,
Cambridge.
Mackenzie, Duncan (1861-1934).
University of Vienna.
Marshall, John Hubert (1876-1958). King's,
Cambridge.
Mayor, Robert John Grote (1869-1947).
King's, Cambridge.
Milne, Joseph Grafton (1867-1951). Corpus
Christi, Oxford.
Morrison, Frederick Arthur Charles (1872-
1899). Jesus, Cambridge.
Moss-Blundell, Cyril Bertram (1891-1915).
New, Oxford.
Munro, John Arthur Ruskin (1864-1944).
Fellow of Lincoln, Oxford.
Myres, John Linton (1869-1954). Fellow of
Magdalen, Oxford.
Oppé, Adolph Paul (1878-1957). New,
Oxford.
Ormerod, Henry Arderne (1886-1964).
Queen's, Oxford.
Orr, Frank George (b. 1881). Glasgow
School of Art.
Parry, Oswald Hutton (1868-1936).
Magdalen, Oxford.
Paterson, Archibald (d. 1932). Edinburgh.
Peet, Thomas Eric (1882-1934). Queen's,
Oxford.
Penoyre, John ffoliot Baker (1870-1954).
Keble, Oxford.
Piddington, John George (J.G. Smith) (b.
1869). Magdalen, Oxford.

Pirie-Gordon, Charles Harry Clinton, of Buthlaw (1883-1969). Magdalen, Oxford.

Radford, Evelyn (1887-1969). Newnham, Cambridge.

Reid, W.W. Aberdeen and Edinburgh.

Reynolds, Edwin Francis (1875-1949).

Richards, George Chatterton (1867-1951). Fellow of Hertford, Oxford.

Richter, Gisela Marie Augusta (1882-1972). Girton, Cambridge.

Robinson, Edward Stanley Gotch (1887-1976). Christ Church, Oxford.

Rodeck, Pieter (b. 1875). Gold Medallist of the Royal Academy.

Rosenörn-Lehn, Baroness E. Royal Holloway College, and University College London.

Schultz Weir, Robert Weir (R.W. Schultz) (1860-1951). Gold Medallist and Travelling Student in Architecture of the Royal Academy of Arts.

Schultz, Robert Weir. *See Schultz Weir, Robert Weir.*

Scutt, Cecil Allison (1889-1961). Clare, Cambridge.

Sellers, Eugénie (Mrs A. Arthur Strong) (1860-1943). Girton, Cambridge.

Sheepshanks, Arthur Charles (1884-1961). Trinity, Cambridge.

Sikes, Edward Ernest (1867-1940). St John's, Cambridge.

Smith, John George. *See Piddington, John George.*

Smith, Ravenscroft Elsey (1859-1930).
RIBA studentship.
Smith, Solomon Charles Kaines (1876-1958). Magdalene, Cambridge.
Spilsbury, Alfred John (1974-1940).
Queen's, Oxford.
Stainer, John Frederick Randall (1866-1939). Magdalen, Oxford.
Stokes, John Laurence (1881-1948).
Pembroke, Cambridge.
Strong, Eugénie. *See Sellers, Eugénie.*
Stuart-Jones, Henry. *See Jones, Henry Stuart.*
Taylor, Mary Norah Luton (Mrs M.N.L. Bradshaw) (1890-1967). Newnham, Cambridge.
Tennant, Lilian Elizabeth (Mrs F.J. Watson-Taylor) (1884-1946).
Thompson, Maurice Scott (1884-1971).
Corpus Christi, Oxford.
Tillard, Laurence Berkley (1888-1943). St John's, Cambridge.
Tillyard, Eustace Mandeville Wetenhall (1889-1962). Jesus, Cambridge.
Tillyard, Henry Julius Wetenhall (1881-1968). Gonville & Caius, Cambridge.
Tod, Marcus Niebuhr (1878-1974). St John's, Oxford.
Toynbee, Arnold Joseph (1889-1975).
Balliol, Oxford.
Traquair, Ramsay (1874-1952).
Architectural studentship.
Tubbs, Henry Arnold (b. 1865). Pembroke, Oxford.

Wace, Alan John Bayard (1879-1957).
Pembroke, Cambridge.
Watson-Taylor, Lilian Elizabeth. *See
Tennant, Lilian Elizabeth.*
Webster, Erwin Wentworth (1880-1917).
Wadham, Oxford.
Welch, Francis Bertram (1876-1950).
Magdalen, Oxford.
Wells, Robert Douglas (1875-1963). Trinity,
Cambridge.
Welsh, Margery Katharine (Mrs A. M.
Daniel) (1880-1960). Newnham,
Cambridge.
West, Hercules Henry (1856-1937). Trinity,
Cambridge.
Whatley, Norman (1884-1965). Fellow of
Hertford College, Oxford.
Wigram, Rev. William Ainger (1872-1953).
Trinity Hall, Cambridge.
Woodhouse, William John (1866-1937).
Queen's, Oxford.
Woodward, Arthur Maurice (1883-1973).
Magdalen, Oxford.
Yorke, Vincent Wodehouse (1869-1957).
King's, Cambridge.

www.ingramcontent.com/pod-product-compliance
Lightning Source LLC
Chambersburg PA
CBHW051636050426
42443CB00024B/301